THE LOCH NESS MONSTER

Charles Fowkes

FACT OR FOLKLORE?

Situated in the Scottish Highlands, Loch Ness is an awe-inspiring place with a mystery lurking in its gloomy depths: the Loch Ness Monster.

Belief in the reality of the elusive monster has persisted for nearly 1,400 years, from the Dark Ages to the present day, and through the centuries 'Nessie' (*Niseag* in Gaelic) – as the monster is affectionately known – has stubbornly refused to be dismissed as fiction. Modern science and technology have, if anything, deepened and complicated the mystery.

There are many possible explanations for the world-famous phenomenon, and 21st-century research benefits from the analytical tools at our disposal: modern zoology, wave physics, anthropology and psychology, supported by photo analysis, state-of-the-art imaging techniques, sonar and the latest developments in DNA sampling. Vital to the continuing search are the first-hand accounts of those individuals who claim to have seen the Loch Ness Monster and are in no doubt that Nessie does exist. Last but not least is the intrepid band of loners and eccentrics – the monster hunters.

Searching for Nessie in Loch Ness inevitably takes people into some dark places. All of them – from the scientific expert to the hopeful tourist – can be applauded for their perseverance and for giving hope to all lovers of mysteries.

THE LARGEST
LAKE IN BRITAIN

Loch Ness is unique – a vast body of freshwater, with an estimated volume
of 7 billion cubic metres, making it the largest lake in Britain. The loch is 39
kilometres long, stretching from Lochend at its northernmost point to Fort
Augustus in the south. The steep sides of the loch and the gaunt crags and
precipices give an impression of pressing in on one another above the surface
of the water. The average width of Loch Ness is 1.5 kilometres and its waters
very deep, plunging down to 228 metres, and 244 metres in the abyss by
Urquhart Castle on its westerly coast.

The variation in colour and wave pattern of the lake surface gives Loch Ness
its changing moods: deep azure under a bright blue summer sky can quickly
change to inky black under dark clouds. The lake is cold: below 30 metres
a more or less constant 5.5 degrees Celsius, although at the surface in
summertime the temperature can approach 10–14 degrees Celsius. The
water – brown because of the high peat content – plunges into darkness
below 8 or 9 metres with zero visibility.

If some dark pagan deity set out to design the ideal environment for an
elusive monster to live and have its being, it would be Loch Ness.

MYSTERIES &
SYMBOLISM

Human beings like mysteries: we are fascinated by those things at the edge of our understanding. Mythology – our earliest stories and visual art – is filled with monsters, creatures from the unknown that may, or may not, threaten us. They are everywhere: in literature, in cinema and in folklore – the beliefs and stories which people of all cultures hand down through the generations. Often monster stories have some basis in reality. In Jules Verne's science fiction novel *Twenty Thousand Leagues Under the Sea*, the Giant Squid which attacks the submarine *Nautilus* falls into the category of unlikely but not impossible. It bears some resemblance to the serpentine monster described by Aristotle in the 4th century BC. This hazard to Greek shipping is said to have capsized a trireme, the most powerful war and trading ship of the period. The famous Kraken (main picture) of Norse legend, which devoured Viking ships, exhibited the same anti-social behaviour. The new technology used in David Attenborough's

'Of course the
Loch Ness
Monster exists:
it exists in our
Collective
Unconscious.'

Anonymous Jungian analyst

> '**The inexpressible can only be expressed in terms of symbols and myth …**'
>
> Carl Gustav Jung

2017 documentary series *Blue Planet II* shows how much science has yet to learn about the ocean depths and the creatures that live there.

In contrast to the vastness of the seas or oceans, inland lakes are part of our human landscape. A lake is also an alien world to terrestrial *Homo sapiens*, but the relationship to these bodies of water is more intimate. We live by lakes, we fish them and have the opportunity to observe them constantly, and out of what we see (or think we see) we weave stories and myths. In addition to its physical reality as a barrier to be crossed and a source of food, a lake has a symbolic value. The mood of a lake changes as it mirrors the sky, and in the myths mankind creates its depths are often seen as portals to another world, a realm that is unseen and unknown. Lakes are often dangerous, too, life-threatening and sinister. Unlike the rivers which feed them, the life-current in a lake does not flow, it is contained.

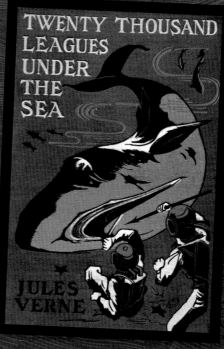

RIGHT: Twenty Thousand Leagues Under the Sea – *a classic tale of underwater mystery.*

WORMS & MONSTERS

Nessie may be the most famous lake monster in the world, and probably the most documented, but whatever it is the Loch Ness Monster is not a unique phenomenon.

Lagarfljót Worm

Far north of the Scottish Highlands, in Iceland there is a monster with a curiously similar career to Nessie: the Lagarfljót Worm, which has many parallels in the phenomenon of the Loch Ness Monster. It has been sighted on several occasions in modern times – notably by the Head of the Icelandic National Forest Service, and by a teacher and a group of students – and videos of the Worm have been broadcast. The first recorded Worm sighting dates from 1345: 'a wonderful thing'; a map of 1585 shows Lagarfljót with the inscription 'in this lake appears a large serpent'; and in 1638 a bishop writes of a 'strandvorm'. Over its long history the Worm has been observed out of water, either coiled up or slithering into the trees, and has been assessed to be 12 metres long with several humps. All the usual scientific explanations have been put forward but the Worm still returns.

American and Canadian monsters

In the USA sightings of mysterious lake monsters have been recorded in numerous states. Among the most persistent is Old Greeny in Cayuga Lake, Ithaca, NY, for which sightings began in 1828 after the lake was connected to the Erie Canal. Other monsters have a much longer lineage and appear in the legends of Native American peoples. The same is true of Canada which has many lake monsters, with perhaps the most famous being the Nennorluk in Labrador, Newfoundland, and the Ogopogo in Lake Okanagan in British Columbia. In the 1870s a Mrs Allison described a sighting: 'My mother did tell us about seeing the Ogopogo in a storm ... going against the current, not with it.'

Monsters around the world

A similar pattern of folklore tradition, reinforced with modern sightings of monsters or worms, has been recorded in numerous other places including China, Japan, Thailand, Russia, Turkey and most European countries. In Africa, Lake Tanganyika, Lake Victoria and others have added to the record of monster sightings: some of these have been attributed to the Vundu catfish (main picture) which can grow to a gigantic size. It is interesting that a contemporary theory in anthropology attributes the significant increase in brain size and intelligence that occurred in our hominid ancestors in Africa's Rift Valley to the consumption of stranded catfish, a species rich in the brain-food Omega 3 oil. With intelligence comes imagination…

Other British monsters

Nessie's closer relatives include the Bassenthwaite Lake Monster in the Lake District and Morag in Loch Morar. Unlike Loch Ness, Loch Morar is crystal clear and at 310 metres is deeper than Loch Ness, but is a similarly magical place with a long history of monster sightings. The 1972 book *The Search for Morag* by Elizabeth Montgomery Campbell contains a warning to the curious in the form of a traditional poem:

Morag, Harbinger of Death,
Giant swimmer in deep green Morar,
The loch that has no bottom …
There it is that Morag the monster lives.

LOCH NESS: HAUNTED BY A DRAGON?

Dragons are popular in human culture: in children's books, in heraldry, in the Bible, in myths and legends throughout the world. Fictional dragons are sometimes charming, but the dragons of myth and legend rarely so.

Most people can describe what a dragon looks like, despite having never seen a real one. Early man, however, would have been familiar with the bones of dinosaurs which are abundant in Jurassic soil, so perhaps it was through these giant lizards that the 'dragon' entered the human unconscious.

The physical attributes of this creature of the imagination are variable according to tradition, but images of dragons tend to show them as green, scaly and associated with water. The Greek word *drakon* also means 'serpent'.

Dragons as symbols

Legendary dragons have been known to breathe fire and protect hidden treasure. In China and Japan dragons are mainly positive and benevolent but the Old Testament of the Bible takes the opposite view, identifying the creature as the Devil or Devil's servant. For psychologist Carl Gustav Jung, the dragon is a symbol representing the negative and devouring mother-image – a concept which would have shocked intrepid dragon slayers like Siegfried and St George, heroes of ancient legend.

Kelpies

Long before the Viking raiders, in their dragon-prowed ships, brought fire and terror to Scotland, the Celtic inhabitants of the Highlands lived in awe of kelpies. These supernatural creatures (also known as water horses) were malicious and had a lust for human flesh. Supernatural explanations of the Loch Ness Monster are – together with many mainstream religious beliefs – beyond the realm of science.

Aleister Crowley

The notorious Aleister Crowley (left) of black magic fame bought Boleskine House above Loch Ness together with a stretch of shoreline. The self-styled 'wickedest man in the world' lived by the essential tenet of the cult he formed: 'Do what thou wilt shall be the whole of the law.' For Crowley this involved every kind of excess. In his world of 'Magick' the Loch Ness Monster is seen as a powerful Elemental, a creature of water and darkness. We will never know what dark purposes Crowley might have had for Nessie or what primordial powers he hoped to harness in his 13 years living there.

'I believe in everything until it's disproved. So I believe in fairies, the myths, dragons. It all exists, even if it's in your mind.'

John Lennon

Zoology, biology and the physical sciences provide their own rational explanations of the Loch Ness Monster phenomenon, which countless individuals claim to have experienced for themselves and others have famously photographed, filmed and imaged with sonar equipment.

Dinosaurs

Early photographs (some of them known to be hoaxes) have supported and fed the idea that Nessie is an unknown species, perhaps a relic from the Age of Dinosaurs (like the coelacanth which was absent from the fossil record for 65 million years until it was discovered 1938). This creature would need to have been tenacious of life as Loch Ness was frozen for 20,000 years during the last Ice Age and only became the body of water we now see around 10,000 years ago. After the great melt the lake was saline at first, gradually changing to fresh water as newly formed rivers flowed into it. Nevertheless, 'Nessie the orphan dinosaur' remains a popular idea and it is human nature to see what we expect to see: long necks, flippers etc. Other creatures already recorded by zoologists may also have played their part in the Loch Ness story.

Fish

In 1661 a giant sturgeon was seen in the river at Inverness: it measured nearly 3 metres in length. In the 19th century, catfish were introduced to Loch Ness, a species which can grow to a gigantic size with a good food source and an absence of predators (as in Lake Klopein in Austria). Other fish species are abundant in Loch Ness, including Arctic char (a real relic of the Ice Age) and

RIGHT: *Sturgeons can grow enormous and easily be mistaken for a monster.*

ferrox trout which predate on them, along with other species of trout, and both wild and farmed salmon. Eels (main picture), which are plentiful in the mud at the bottom of the loch, can also grow to an enormous size and occasionally put in an appearance on the surface. The Lampton Worm (and countless other Worm sightings throughout Europe) is probably attributable to sightings of giant eels, with each story being exaggerated and elaborated as is the tendency in folklore.

Otters and seals

These mammals may explain some monster sightings. Otters and seals are surface swimmers and leave a V-shaped wake. Many contemporary webcam sightings can only be explained in this way.

'I hope it's there. But I hope they don't find it – because if they do, they'll do something nasty to it.'

Dr David Bellamy, broadcaster and naturalist

THE UNNATURAL
WORLD

The other mammal which has confused the picture is ourselves, *Homo sapiens*. Hoaxers and jokers have further muddied the already murky waters of Loch Ness, for example, with such escapades as the 'muddy footprints' episode of the 1930s. In reality these were the imprint of what was probably an ashtray or umbrella stand made from a hippopotamus foot: as a contemporary zoologist noted, 'strange enough in itself, but a one-legged hippo?!'

During filming of the 1970 movie *The Private Life of Sherlock Holmes* a 'life-size' replica of the dinosaur lookalike Nessie (main picture) was lost and presumably still lurks at the bottom of the loch – a joke which must have amused star of the film Christopher Lee and director Billy Wilder.

Another amusing incident involved Bertram Mills and his travelling circus. Not only did Mills encourage monster hunters by offering a reward for Nessie's capture, he is said to have allowed elephants to swim in Loch Ness. A submerged elephant with a humped back and its trunk sticking out of the water gives a good impression of a classic monster sighting.

Logs

Resinous pine logs decay very slowly; gases form and may eventually propel a long, dark body to the surface with startling results. This phenomenon has been recorded at Lake Toplitz in Austria, famed for being where, during the Second World War, the Nazis tried to conceal filing cabinets with details of their genocidal crimes and printing plates of counterfeit pound notes intended to weaken the British economy.

Methane gas

Occasional eruptions of gas from decaying vegetable matter at the bottom of Loch Ness may account for sightings of disturbances in the water and unexplained sonar recordings.

> 'Now I am become Death, the destroyer of worlds.'
>
> from the Hindu script *Bhagavad-Gita*, quoted by J. Robert Oppenheimer, 'father' of the atomic bomb

Submarines

Submarines of various kinds have been used to search for the Loch Ness Monster. In 1969 the Vickers Oceanic's submersible *Pisces* made contact with a large object 15 metres off the bottom. In 1969 a private submarine, *Viperfish*, was built by an American, Dan Taylor, but defeated by poor visibility. But there is an earlier submarine story. The son of a family with estates in the Highlands served in Naval Intelligence in the Second World War; he remembered a file on Loch Ness compiled during the arms race period leading up to the First World War when top secret prototype submarines were tested in the loch on several occasions. The file detailed security arrangements and a strategy of misinformation based on the age-old local belief that there is something strange in the loch. The deception was, of course, designed to explain unexpected bow waves and turbulence. The Security Services have now switched their attention to Gare Loch (Faslane) in western Scotland, which is the base for the Royal Navy's fleet of nuclear submarines and Britain's principal nuclear deterrent.

RIGHT: *A nuclear submarine – these ominous machines have history in the loch.*

HIDDEN DEPTHS: WAVES & SEICHES

Watching the wave patterns on the surface of Loch Ness (either from above or at the lakeside) can be a mesmerizing experience. The loch lies in the Great Glen, a geological fault seen running top right to bottom left, as seen in the map to the right. This runs NE–SW and acts as a wind tunnel for the prevailing south westerly winds. Locals sometimes call Loch Ness 'the sea' (reminiscent of the German word for lake, *See*) and in strong winds the serried ranks of waves have something of the sea about them. But below the surface other, more powerful, hidden forces are at work.

Seiches are underwater waves. Warmer surface water forms a layer which sits on the permanently cold (5.5 degrees Celsius) deep water. This interface is the thermocline. The seiches or waves of the thermocline have a rhythm of their own, moving vast volumes of water (millions of tons). These seiches move up and down the lake like a perpetual motion machine. There are sonar recordings of a 40-metre high underwater wave. Unseen, below the surface, these seiches have a dramatic effect on the surface dynamic of the loch. These effects may account for some sightings where the 'monster' seems to move against the prevailing current. Seiches also create sonar anomalies known as underwater mirages. These are not fully understood but they sometimes have serpentine shapes.

The wake effect

There are times when the surface of Loch Ness is calm. It was this characteristic which prompted John Cobb (left – land speed record holder) to attempt the water speed record in 1952. Snatching the opportunity of a very calm day on 29 September, the jet boat *Crusader* and its support vessel moved into place but sadly they had underestimated the persistence of their own wakes. When *Crusader* hit these at 200 miles per hour, the boat disintegrated and Cobb was killed. The unexpected persistence of wakes on Loch Ness, even after the vessel causing them has long gone, are thought to account for some monster sightings.

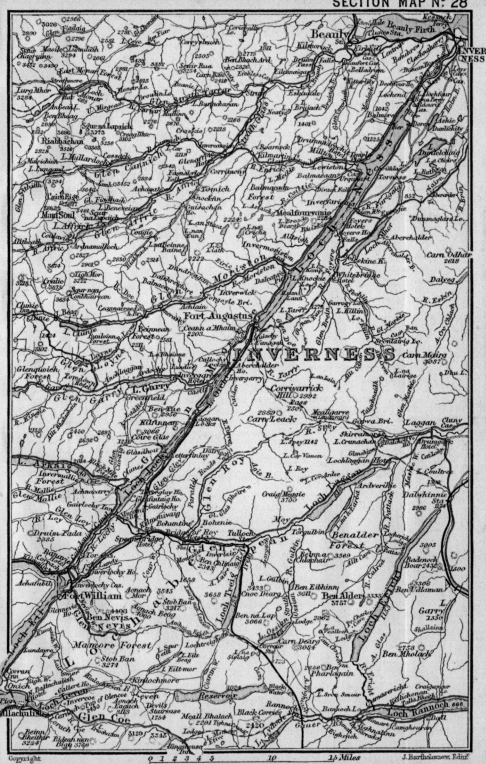

ROADS, CANALS & THE AGE OF TOURISM

The Great Glen in which Loch Ness lies provides the Highlands with a natural corridor. During the 1745 rebellion, ending in the bloody defeat of the Highlanders at Culloden, General Wade (1673–1747) built a road along the southern shore of Loch Ness linking Fort Augustus and Inverness (see Gaelic Place Names & Meanings, *1, at the back of the book).
General Wade's military roads linked the garrisons at Ruthven, Fort George, Fort Augustus and Fort William. This verse is attributed to Wade's successor, Major William Caulfeild:
'If you had seen this road before it was made,
You would lift up your hands and bless General Wade.'

Caledonian Canal

Water-borne traffic increased hugely after the construction of the Caledonian Canal in 1822 (main picture). Thomas Telford's (1757–1834) remarkable engineering feat, a 60-mile [97-kilometre] canal linking two seas, failed to impress Queen Victoria on her inaugural voyage along the its length: she found it 'rather tedious'. Canal traffic led to some increase in monster sightings.

Motor transport

General Wade's military road was soon screened from the loch by trees and the road on the north side was a tortuous mule track. The advent of motorized transport in the first decades of the 20th century meant that a new road had to be blasted through the rock with dynamite. Some locals believed that blasting accounted for the sudden increase in monster sightings, as if Nessie had been disturbed by the shocks. But of course there were also many more people looking at the lake. To cater for fishermen and other visitors, hotels and other facilities grew up: the Age of Tourism had begun.

Monsters in the Bible

Sea monsters (Leviathan) and dragons appear many times in the Bible: 'Leviathan the piercing serpent, even Leviathan the crooked serpent; and he shall slay the dragon that is in the sea.' (Isiah 27.1). These creatures are the enemies of the righteous and include snakes and the Nile crocodile, a reptile which the Israelites learned to fear during their captivity in Egypt.

SIGHTINGS & RESEARCH:
Chronological List

It is 10,000 years since the Melting of the Ice and the repopulation of the Great Geological Fault which bisects what is now Scotland. Modern man is much older than that, of course, and human migration is not a recent invention: it is what humankind does. Change is our destiny as each successive wave of people brings something new. For most of human history, 'monsters' – everything we did not know, could not understand and feared – were part of everyday life. In the secret, enclosed lochs where life clings to the edges, we are – whether we like it or not – still in the realm of the sea creature. That is the genius loci: the spirit of the place.

On the following pages is a timeline of events, from the earliest times to the present day, listing the findings or otherwise of those who have seen or searched for the mystery that is the Loch Ness Monster.

Asterisked references (e.g. *1) can be found under Gaelic Place Names & Meanings at the back of the book.

565 – St Columba

The famous incident of St Columba and the Monster has some unique features that make it important. Born in County Donegal in Ireland of royal blood, Columba was as impressive physically as he was intellectually and spiritually. By winning the approval of the Druid priest Oran he was able to found the Christian monastic community on Iona which exists to this day. Pictish tribesmen had a unique language and art distinct from the Celts, and are thought to have been the 'aboriginal' inhabitants of the Highlands. Stone circles, tumuli and snake-path shrines in the area indicate the persistence of the pagan beliefs with which the Christian missionary Columba had to contend.

The monster incident is faithfully described in Latin by Adamnan, Columba's successor as Abbot of Iona. The 'good and wise' Adamnan, knowing that his account would be suspect for bias, preceded it with the words 'let no-one suspect any falsehood or anything doubtful or uncertain in this record'.

In crossing the River Ness at the eastern end of the loch, Columba came upon the body of an unfortunate local who had been attacked by a monster and died of his injuries. One of Columba's followers dived bravely into the water and was immediately pursued by the monster which had been lurking unseen below the surface. In the panic which ensued the saint's voice rang out, 'Go no further nor touch that man: go back at once ... I exorcise you, creature of water!', banishing the creature (in the manner of an exorcism) back to the deep. The monster clearly understood its part in the drama and obeyed.

'I exorcise you, creature of water...'

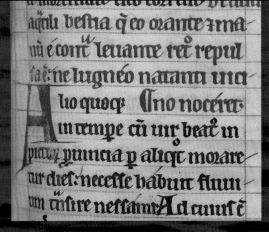

1527 – Duncan Campbell

Mr Campbell saw a 'terrible beast' on the loch shore.

16th century – Chronicle

Report of gigantic monster coming out of Loch Ness, savaging three men.

17th century – English chronicler

Richard Franck, a Cromwellian soldier who visited Loch Ness in the 17th century, writes in his *Northern Memoirs* that Loch Ness was renowned for its mysterious 'swimming islands'.

October 1871 or 1872 – D. Mackenzie

Although it took some 60 years for the following eyewitness account to be made public, it is an interesting addition to the evidence for something large and animate in Loch Ness. In its way this account stands for the countless unrecorded sightings, which took place over centuries:

'... I saw it about 1871 or 1872, as near as I can remember now. I was on *the rock above Abriachan (*2), taking home bracken in October, when I saw what I took to be a log of wood coming across the Loch from the Aldourie (*3) side. The water was very calm at the time. I expected it to go down the Loch towards the river (the River Ness, at the Northern end of Loch Ness). However when it reached the middle of the Loch it suddenly appeared to come to life. It looked like an upturned boat, and went at great speed, wriggling and churning up the water, in the direction of Urquhart Castle. It was about 12 o'clock on a grand sunny day, so that it was impossible for me to be mistaken. It was an animal of some sort; and I have told this same story to my friends long before the present monster became famous …'*

1879 – Group of children

A group of children saw a 'small head on a long neck' on the north shore.

1895 – The Duke of Portland

When the Duke of Portland became the tenant for the salmon angling in Loch Oich and the River Garry in 1895, he records in his diary that the forester and fishing ghillies often used to talk about a horrible great 'beasty' which appeared in Loch Ness.

1916 – James Cameron

Head keeper of the Balmacaan estate walked into the Drumnadrochit (*4) Hotel with 'his face as white as paper'. Cameron said that while he was fishing from a small boat on the loch an 'enormous animal'

had surfaced very near him. The shock caused him to become dizzy and he rowed ashore as quickly as he could.

April 1923 – Alfred Cruickshank

Cruickshank saw a long animal with a bent back and four elephant-like feet crossing the road in front of his car.

27 August 1930 – Fishermen

First modern newspaper report in the *Northern Chronicle*: 'Fishermen in boat disturbed by 6m long creature.'

1933 – Reward for catching monster

Bertram Mills, the famous circus owner, offered a £20,000 reward for anyone who could catch the newly christened monster. the New York Zoological Park added a further £5,000.

2 May 1933 – Alex Campbell and Mr and Mrs MacKay

Alex Campbell – water bailiff at Fort Augustus and part-time journalist (who claimed that he had seen the monster himself) – uses the term 'Loch Ness Monster' for the first time in an article in the *Inverness Courier*. He reported that Mr and Mrs MacKay of Drumnadrochit saw something strange in the loch near Abriachan:

'a whale-like fish'

'A violent commotion in the water … a wake caused by something big below the surface … black humps rising and sinking … a whale-like fish.'

22 July 1933 – Mr and Mrs George Spicer

Londoner George Spicer and his wife reported seeing the 'nearest approach to a dragon or pre-historic animal' trundling across the road with an animal in its mouth. Sightings increased after road improvements. More letters of sightings appeared in the *Courier* and international interest grew: the *Daily Mail*, *The Scotsman*, *Le Matin de Paris* and two Japanese papers all send reporters to Loch Ness.

August 1933 – Mr and Mrs McLennan

Another out-of-water sighting. The monster was seen resting on the shore not far from where Mr and Mrs Spicer saw it.

11 August 1933, 7am – A. H. Palmer

Mr Palmer's sighting was remarkable for the cosmetic detail about the head and mouth of the monster.

20 October 1933 – *Scott II* (Caledonian Ship Canal)

Group sighting from crewmen of a tug and barge. Engineer R. McConnell was convinced it was neither a whale nor a seal. He and his mate Mr Cameron saw about 8 feet [2.5 metres] of the creature's back. It made a V-shaped wave.

November 1933 – Rupert Thomas Gould

Commander Gould RN, a polymath and enthusiast, toured the loch on his motorbike 'Cynthia' interviewing more than 50 people who had seen something unusual. He concluded that the monster was a large living creature with a long body and snake-like head: 'No other theory can be advanced which covers the whole of the facts.'

12 November 1933 – Hugh Gray

Local man Hugh Gray took first photograph of the monster close to the mouth of the River Foyers (*5).

SEEN BY MR. & MRS. MACLENNAN FROM A BOAT IN JUNE, 1933 - DISTANCE ABOUT 400 YARDS - "MONSTER" JUST OFF TEMPLE PIER, DRUMNADROCHIT. (FROM A DRAWING MADE UNDER THEIR SUPERVISION)

THE MACLENNANS' SKETCH

TEN OTHER WITNESSES FROM SEPTEMBER 22ND, 1933, 11AM

LEFT: *August 1933 – An artist's sketch of Mr and Mrs McLennan's sighting.*

6 December 1933 – Gray's photo published

Hugh Gray's picture was published in the *Daily Express/Daily Sketch* with a note from Kodak stating that the negative had not been tampered with in any way. The original negative has been lost. Maurice Burton (the British zoologist and science author) said he obtained positives from the original negative, which seemed to show an otter.

1934: *Mr Arthur Grant.*

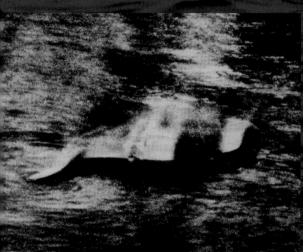

1933: *Hugh Gray's photograph.*

December 1933 – Footprint hoax

The *Daily Mail* sponsored a Loch Ness Hunt expedition. Big game hunter Marmaduke Wetherell and his assistant Gustave Pauli claimed to have found tracks in the mud. In fact it was a joke, using a tourist trophy made from a hippo foot.

Late 1933 – First movie pictures

Malcolm Irvine of Scottish Film Productions filmed a moving object opposite Urquhart Castle. Irvine shot further footage in 1936

5 January 1934 – Arthur Grant

While riding his motorcycle near Abriachan (north-east end of the loch), Arthur Grant, a veterinary student, reported swerving to avoid hitting the creature.

19 April 1934 – Robert Kenneth Wilson: 'the surgeon'

First picture of Nessie's head and neck. London gynaecologist Robert Kenneth Wilson supposedly took a picture of the monster, then distanced himself from the ensuing furore. The iconic image came to be known as 'the surgeon's photograph'.

17 June 1934 – Loch Ness Field Club

Sighting by members of the Loch Ness Field Club which included an ex provost and the Registrar for the Burgh. The official report said:

'At first they thought it might be a piece of debris but this theory had to be discarded when they realised that it was travelling against the current.'

8 August 1934 – Sir Murdoch Macdonald

Sir Murdoch Macdonald KCMG (1866–1957) reported a new sighting: 'At first it was almost still ... but had a slow motion towards Fort Augustus.' A fellow passenger exclaimed, 'By Jove, the Monster!' A pragmatic Scot who had advised on the defence of the Suez Canal in the First World War, Sir Murdoch was not given to flights of fancy.

Summer 1934 – Sir Edward Mountain's Loch Ness Expedition

After reading Rupert Gould's *Loch Ness Monster and Others*, Sir Edward Mountain (1872–1948), founder of Eagle Star Insurance (who famously refused to insure RMS *Titanic*), financed an expedition of 20 unemployed local men and Supervisor/ Captain James Fraser. Fraser shot some film footage on 15 September 1934. Sadly the film has been lost.

15 August 1938 – William Fraser

The Chief Constable of Inverness-shire, William Fraser, wrote a letter to the authorities on monster hunters, which was finally released by the National Archives of Scotland on 27 April 2010.

July 1951 – Lachlan Stuart

Lachlan Stuart, a woodsman, photographed something with three humps.

December 1954 – Sonar readings

Fishing boat *Rival III* took sonar readings; crew noted large object keeping pace with vessel at a depth of 480 feet [146 metres].

1934: *The surgeon's famous photograph.*

1955: *McNab's photograph.*

29 July 1955 – Peter MacNab

Photographer P. A. MacNab photographed two long black humps close to Urquhart Castle. First published in Mrs Constance Whyte's (wife of manager of Caledonian Ship Canal) 1957 book: *More Than a Legend*. Photograph also published by the *Weekly Scotsman* on 23 October 1958.

Autumn 1958 – H. L. Cockrell

What is known as the Cockrell Picture showed a hump estimated to be about 4 feet [1.2 metres] long; published in Tim Dinsdale's book *The Story of the Loch Ness Monster*.

Spring 1960 – Torquil Macleod

Macleod reported viewing the monster through binoculars, assessing the creature, which was lying on the rocky edge of the loch, to be between 45 and 55 feet [13–16 metres] long.

Summer 1960 – Mr R. H. Lowrie

Picture taken from deck of the yacht *Finola*, published in Tim Dinsdale's book. The Lowrie photograph showed a V-shaped wash on glassy-calm water, and the monster was described as 'huge and sinister'.

1960 – Tim Dinsdale

Aeronautical engineer Tim Dinsdale filmed a large hump travelling through water at speed. The film was shown on Richard Dimbleby's *Panorama* programme, seen by nearly 10 million people: 'I could see now that it was the back of a great animal ... a strange, humped back ... huge and sinister ... it zig-zagged across the loch, gradually submerging.' Subsequent photographic analysis cast some doubt on the footage, suggesting that it may have been the result of atmospheric distortion.

'huge and sinister'

1962 – Oxford/Cambridge

Strong echo sounder traces (stronger than that produced by salmon) – evidence not conclusive.

1962 – Sir Peter Scott

Sir Peter Scott – naturalist, artist and son of the Antarctic explorer – and others formed the Loch Ness Phenomena Investigation Bureau (LNPIB). Team Leader David James meticulously recorded 258 sightings over a 10-year period.

1963 – Hugh Ayton

Three large humps and neck seen by Mr Ayton of Balachladaich (*6) Farm and three others. They rowed out into the loch, started the motor and followed the monster for about a mile [1.6 kilometres].

15 June 1965 – Ian Cameron

Retired police officer Ian Cameron was fishing on the south shore of Loch Ness with his friend Willie Frazer in June 1965 when he saw something rise out of the water, then disappear: 'Soon, an enormous black animal shot up from below. The creature looked like a cross between an elephant and a whale ... I saw it, and nothing can take that away!' Though the water was flowing in the opposite direction, the giant creature was steadily heading towards the men. Cameron's son, Willie, who has a hotel at the loch, said that his father 'felt as if he was drawn to it ... there was no fear, nothing at all'. There were said to be nine witnesses who corroborated his story.

'I saw it, and nothing can take that away'

1966: *The Loch Ness Phenomena Investigation Bureau (LNPIB).*

1969: *Dan Taylor and others with the* Viperfish.

D.S.T.

⌐L WORLD BOOK ENCYCLOPEDIA
AFFILIATED WITH
The Loch Ness Phenomena Investigation Bureau Ltd.
Loch Ness, Scotland

1967 – Richard (Dick) Raynor

While working for the LNPIB in 1962–72, Raynor took film footage of a moving object.

1967–68 – Sonar studies

D. Gordon Tucker, Chair of the Department of Electronic and Electrical Engineering at the University of Birmingham, volunteered his services as a sonar engineer and collaborated with LNPIB. Sonar device fixed underwater at Temple Pier in Urquhart Bay.

1968 – Further sonar studies

The University of Birmingham brought a more powerful sonar scanner to the loch, situated at Urquhart Bay, working in cooperation with the LNPIB. They detected many objects, some moving at speeds of up to 10 knots.

1969 – *The Private Life of Sherlock Holmes*

During filming of *The Private Life of Sherlock Holmes*, released in 1970, a dummy of the monster was sunk in the loch. Sonar readings recorded in April 2016 by a Norwegian company found a 9 x 4-metre object on the bottom of Loch Ness. It looked a lot like Nessie, which would likely have amused director Billy Wilder.

1969 – The Viperfish

American Dan Taylor, 28, built the mini-sub *Viperfish* at his parents' home in Atlanta, Georgia. He and other members of the LNPID surveyed the bottom of the loch, where a mysterious current threw up silt clouds and span the vehicle on its axis.

June 1969/August 1972 – Frank Searle

Former soldier Frank Searle moved to Loch Ness in his search for Nessie. He ran a houseboat and exhibition in Lower Foyers supported by a Belgian admirer and 'assistant monster huntress'. Some photographs were the result.

19 October 1971 – Father Gregory Brusey

In the autumn of 1971 Father Gregory Brusey was walking with his friend Roger Pugh in the monastery garden of Fort Augustus Abbey. Brusey said, 'It was a lovely morning, and the sun was warm and the water smooth. And with me was a friend, an organist from London. We suddenly noticed a big commotion about 200 yards out in the water, and then a black neck appeared, about eight inches [20 centimetres] in diameter and seven or eight feet [2 or 2.5 metres] high, followed by a hump. It rose, then dove sideways back into the water. It was not a boat or a log or a fish. It was a different animal.'

'We ought to leave the monster alone'

Father Gregory was for many years the music teacher at the Abbey School and famous for his virtuoso performances on the magnificent Abbey organ installed in 1894. As an ordained priest he knew that his first-hand account of a monster sighting would have a special place in the record and was always touchingly defensive of Nessie: 'We ought to leave the monster alone. In this technological age, we've placed a label on everything. I am a champion of the unknown. Mystery intrigues people and so it should remain.'

1972 – Robert Rines

In 1972, researchers from the Academy of Applied Science, under the supervision of Robert H. Rines, used sonar and underwater photography to search for Nessie. One echo suggested 'a highly flexible laterally flattened tail'. At the same time the camera recorded what appeared to be a rhomboid flipper.

On the basis of this Sir Peter Scott gave Nessie her scientific name, *Nessiteras rhombopterix* ('Ness inhabitant with diamond shaped fin') hoping to add the creature to the British Register of Protected Wildlife. Scottish politician Nicholas Fairbairn suggested it was an anagram of 'Monster Hoax by Sir Peter S'.

Rines' 2001 study produced some further photographic evidence. In his final expedition in 2008 he theorized that the creature had become extinct, possibly due to global warming.

1973 – Adrian Shine on the scene

For four decades naturalist Adrian Shine has been the Loch Ness Monster Hunter *par excellence*. Since 1973 he has devoted himself to a science and technology based search for Nessie. Shine has been a key figure in numerous research projects and the Loch Ness Centre at Drumnadrochit.

1974 – Underwater observation vehicle 'Machan'

Investigation of Loch Ness and Loch Morar – the latter has its own monster and clear water – but results were negative.

1975 – Presentation to both Houses of Parliament

Underwater pictures and other evidence presented to Parliament and the press.

21 May 1977 – Anthony 'Doc' Shiels

Shiels, a magician and psychic, camping next to Urquhart Castle, took pictures of the 'monster'. Shiels' 'monster' becomes known as the 'Loch Ness Muppet'.

30 July 1979 – Alistair Boyd

Alistair Boyd and his wife saw a 'huge hump' surface near Temple Pier. He said, 'I know that thing I saw was not a log, or an otter, or a wave of anything like that. It was a large animal, it came heaving out of the water, something like a whale ... It's the most amazing thing I have ever seen in my life, and if I could spend the rest of my life up here looking for another glimpse of it, I would.'

> 'There's something here that we don't understand ... larger than a fish.'

11 October 1987 – Operation Deepscan

A flotilla of 24 motor launches, covering 60 per cent of the water surface, all equipped with sonar. There were some unexplained sonar echoes – larger than a shark but smaller than a whale – but the reading could not be repeated or verified.

1993 – Project Urquhart

The collaboration of journalist and TV new presenter (now royal correspondent) Nicholas Witchell with the Natural History Museum and Fresh Water Biological Association produced useful scientific research but was inconclusive on Nessie.

July 2003 – BBC research

The BBC carried out an extensive examination of Loch Ness using state-of-the-art sonar technology. No trace of the monster was found.

28 May 2007 – Gordon Holmes

Gordon Holmes, a laboratory technician from Yorkshire, shot a video of a long eel-like object. It was estimated to be 14 metres long and moving at 10 kilometres per hour. Adrian Shine described this as the best footage ever seen.

1987: *Operation Deepscan flotilla.*

26 August 2009 – Jason Cooke

Report in *The Sun* newspaper that Jason Cooke spotted a monster via Google Earth. Magnified it looks more like a small boat.

24 August 2011 – Marcus Atkinson

Boat captain Marcus Atkinson photographed a sonar image of a 1.5 metre-wide object, which followed his vessel for two minutes at a depth of 23 metres.

2 November 2011 – George Edwards

George Edwards, skipper of *Nessie Hunter IV*, took a photograph and on 3 August 2012 claimed it showed Nessie, the monster he had spent 26 years searching for. In 2013 he admitted this was a hoax.

27 August 2013 – David Elder

Tourist David Elder presented a five-minute video of a mysterious wave in the loch.

19 April 2014 – Apple Maps

Two men independently spotted a 'monster' on a satellite image on Apple Maps and informed the Official Loch Ness Monster Fan Club.

2015 – Google Street View

In the 81st anniversary year of 'the surgeon's photograph', Google Street View added a new feature to explore the loch above and below the water.

2018: *DNA sampling with Adrian Shine.*

May/June 2018 – DNA sampling

New Zealand scientist Professor Nick Gemmell, Adrian Shine and a team of scientists used environmental DNA sampling techniques to establish what lives in the loch. Gemmell said, 'I'm going into this thinking it's unlikely there is a monster, but I want to test that hypothesis. What we'll get is a really nice survey of the biodiversity of Loch Ness.'

EXPLORING LOCH NESS

There are many ways to explore Loch Ness. The Visit Scotland website (www.visitscotland.com) is a good place to begin, as are tourist offices where you can find up-to-date details of cruises, fishing trips, places to stay and informative maps showing trails and points of interest.

You can even keep an eye on Loch Ness from afar via the several webcams positioned around the loch.

If travelling to Loch Ness, picnickers and 'slow travellers' are likely to enjoy taking the B862 from Dores to Foyers (the higher road) which looks down on the loch.

The Loch Ness Centre and Exhibition in Drumnadrochit, Inverness is a popular visitor attraction which explores Loch Ness from its beginnings to the present day. See their website for details: www.lochness.com.

If you should happen to see Nessie, The Official Loch Ness Monster Sightings Register would love to hear from you (www.lochnesssightings.com).